JOURNAL

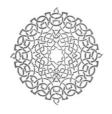

PETER PAUPER PRESS, INC.
WHITE PLAINS, NEW YORK

PETER PAUPER PRESS
Fine Books and Gifts Since 1928

Our Company

In 1928, at the age of twenty-two, Peter Beilenson began printing books on a small press in the basement of his parents' home in Larchmont, New York. Peter—and later, his wife, Edna—sought to create fine books that sold at "prices even a pauper could afford."

Today, still family owned and operated, Peter Pauper Press continues to honor our founders' legacy—and our customers' expectations—of beauty, quality, and value.

Cover art: Qu'ran from El Escorial Library in Madrid,
engraving from El museo español de Antigüedades, 1875
Photo by Kharbine-Tapabor / The Art Archive at Art Resource, NY

Visit us at www.peterpauper.com

9